·I CAN DRAW!·

FavoRite Pets

EMILY FELLAH

Brimming with creative inspiration, how-to projects, and useful information to enrich your everyday life, Quarto Knows is a favorite destination for those pursuing their interests and passions. Visit our site and dig deeper with our books into your area of interest: Quarto Creates, Quarto Cooks, Quarto Homes, Quarto Lives, Quarto Drives, Quarto Explores, Quarto Gifts, or Quarto Kids.

© 2021 Quarto Publishing Group USA Inc.
Text and illustrations © 2021 Emily Fellah

First published in 2021 by Walter Foster Jr., an imprint of The Quarto Group.
26391 Crown Valley Parkway, Suite 220, Mission Viejo, CA 92691, USA.
T (949) 380-7510 **F** (949) 380-7575 **www.QuartoKnows.com**

Walter Foster Jr. titles are also available at discount for retail, wholesale, promotional, and bulk purchase. For details, contact the Special Sales Manager by email at specialsales@quarto.com or by mail at The Quarto Group, Attn: Special Sales Manager, 100 Cummings Center, Suite 265D, Beverly, MA 01915, USA.

ISBN: 978-1-60058-939-3

Digital edition published in 2021
eISBN: 978-1-60058-957-7

Printed in China
10 9 8 7 6 5 4 3 2 1

TABLE OF CONTENTS

HOW TO USE THIS BOOK

Step-by-Step Drawing

This book contains 15 fun drawing projects with step-by-step instructions. Each new step is in color, making it easy to follow along.

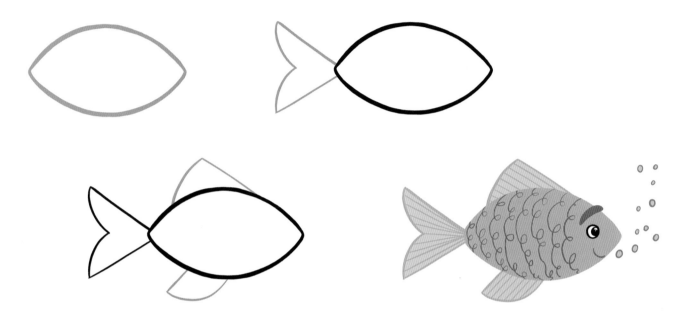

Top Tips

Start lightly in pencil because you will be erasing some of the lines that helped to build your character.

Be careful when erasing because you don't want to crumple or tear your drawing.

If you'd like, you can draw over your finished characters with a fine-line pen or felt-tip marker and erase your pencil lines when the ink is dry.

Tools & Materials

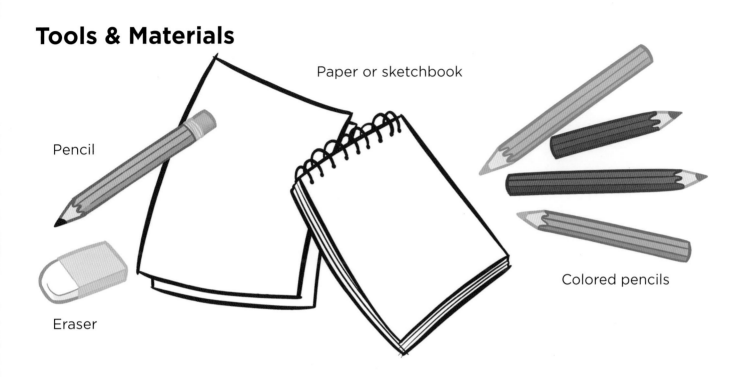

Pencil

Paper or sketchbook

Colored pencils

Eraser

Extras Fine-line pen or felt-tip marker, colored pens, crayons

You Are an Artist!

Your drawings will turn out a little differently from the ones in the book, which is a good thing. You are an individual, and your art will reflect your style and personality, so be proud of it!

PARROT

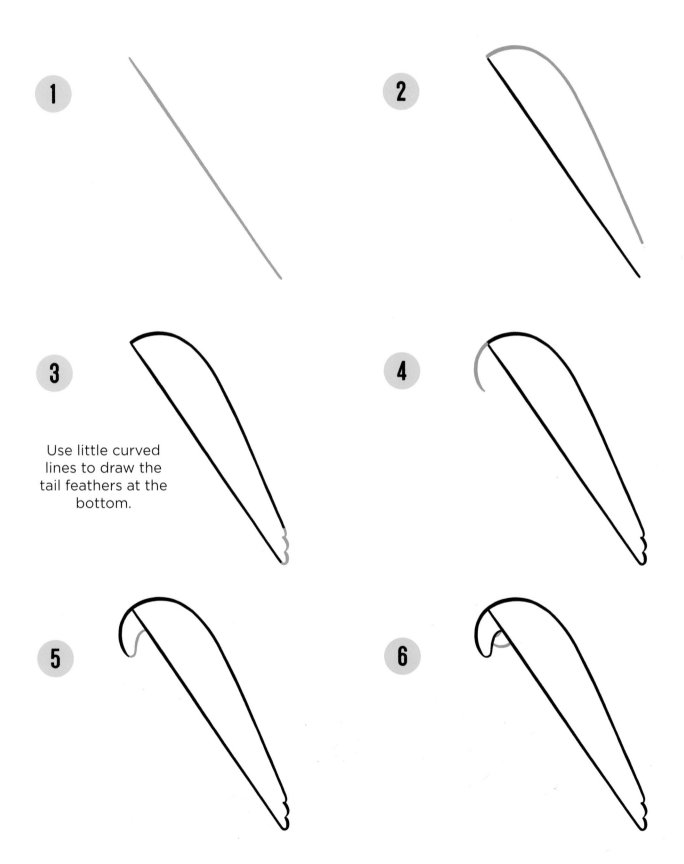

1

2

3

Use little curved lines to draw the tail feathers at the bottom.

4

5

6

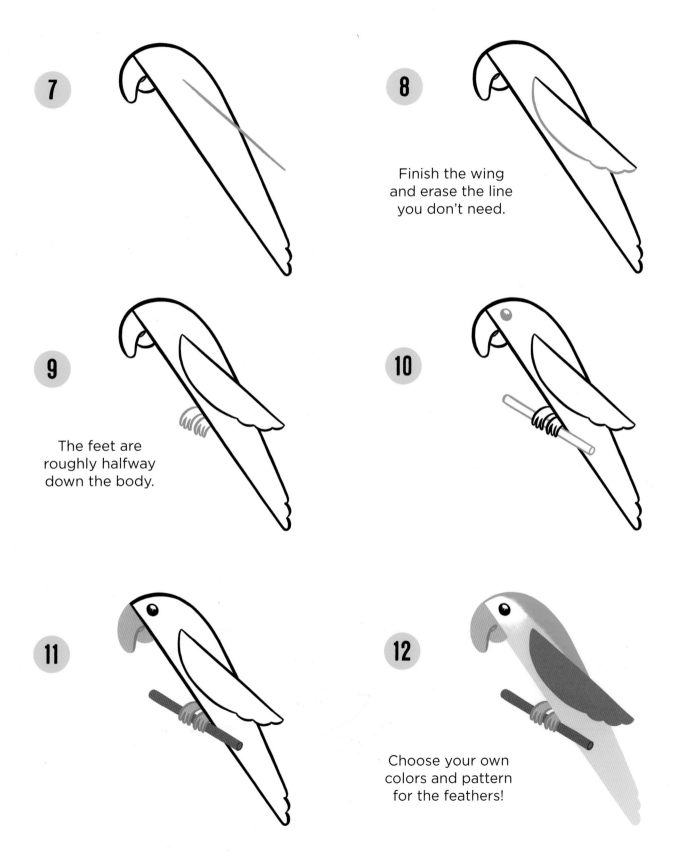

7

8 Finish the wing
and erase the line
you don't need.

9 The feet are
roughly halfway
down the body.

10

11

12 Choose your own
colors and pattern
for the feathers!

FROG

1

2

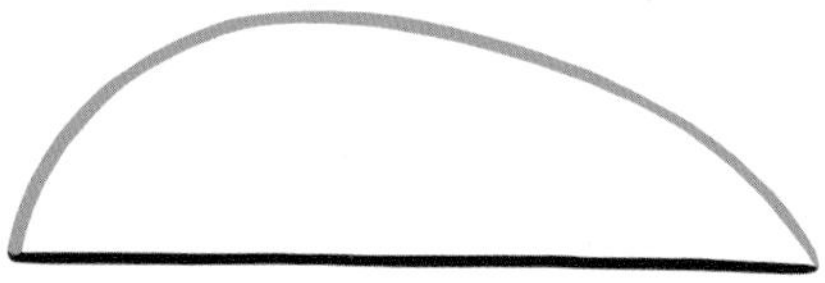

3

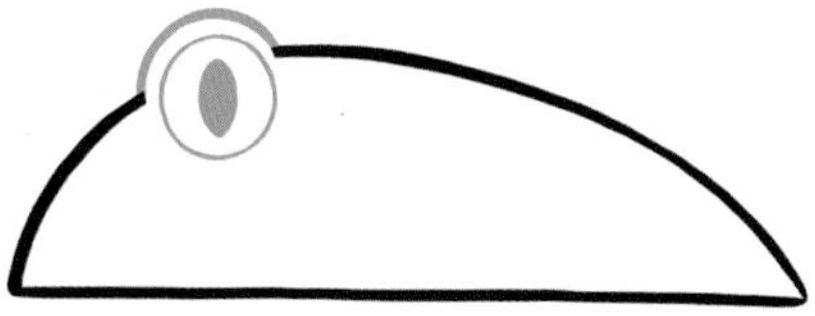

Start with the curve, erase the line you
don't need, and then draw the eye.

4

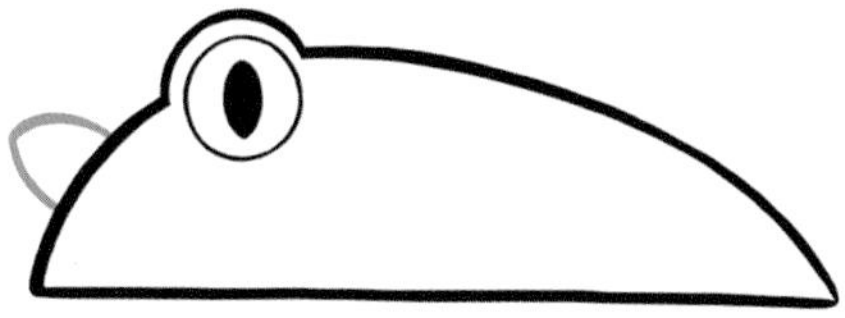

5

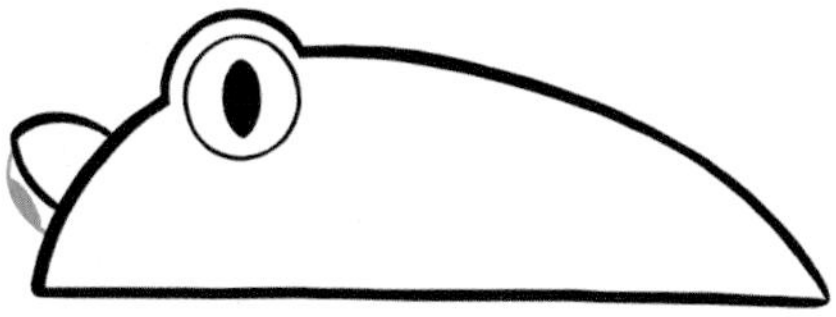

6

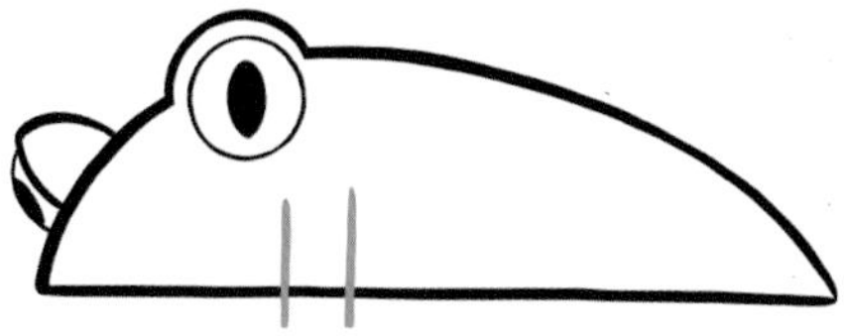

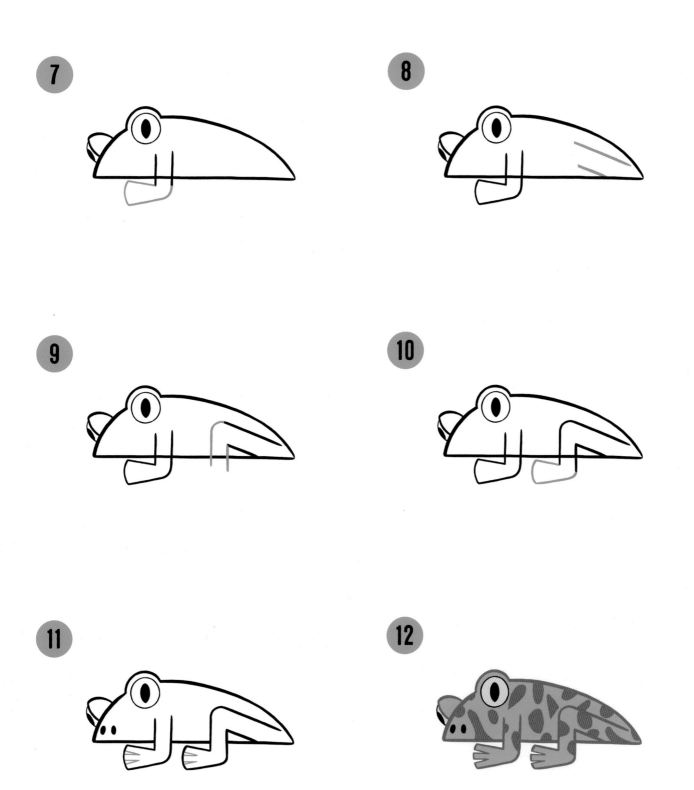

Have fun designing your own markings!

FISH

1

2

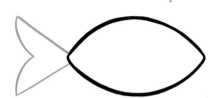

3

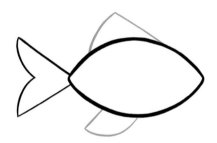

Notice how different these
two fin shapes are.

4

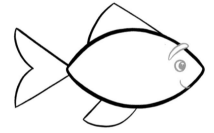

5

Use any pattern you like on
your fish's body.

6

Color the fins in a paler orange
so they look transparent.

GERBIL

1

2

3

After you draw the ears, erase
the lines you don't need.

4

5

6

Draw some furry
lines and color
softly in pencil,
leaving plenty of
white space.

CAT

1

Start by drawing lightly with your pencil because you will erase some of these lines later.

2

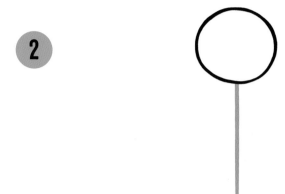

3

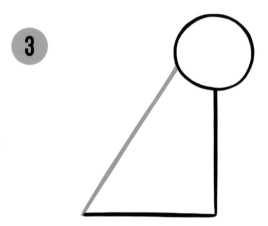

4

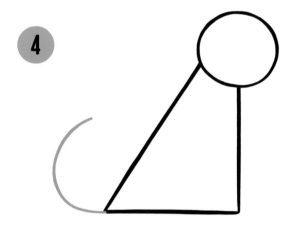

5

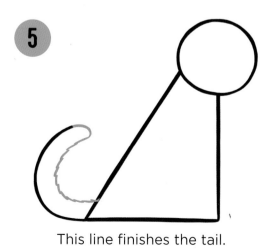

This line finishes the tail.

6

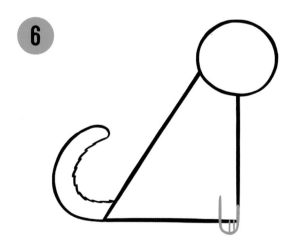

7

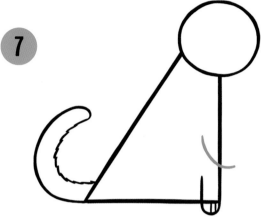

The second leg is tricky,
so take your time.

8

9

10

Erase the lines you don't need
and draw the ears.

11

12

When adding color, remember to
leave some white patches.

LONG-EARED RABBIT

1

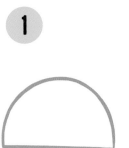

2

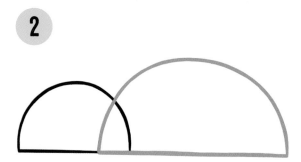

Start by drawing two half circles that overlap.

3

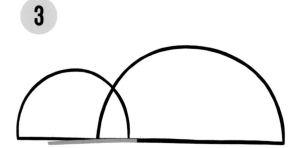

4

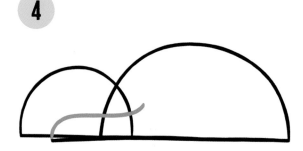

5

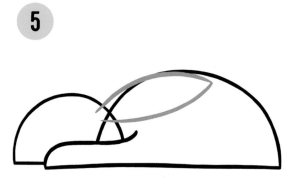

6

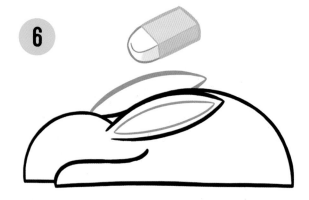

Erase the lines you no longer need and finish the ears.

7

Draw some furry lines in your own style.

8

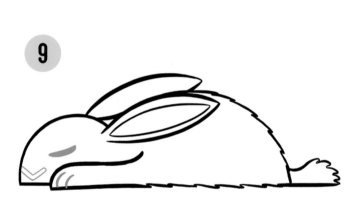

9

10

11

12

z^{z}Z

Decide where you want the patches of color and draw some sleeping ZZZs!

DOG

1

2

3

4 These first few steps are all straight lines.

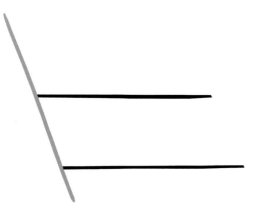

5

6

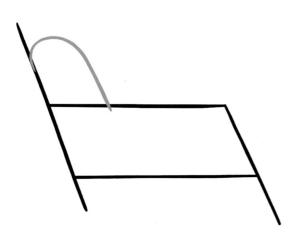

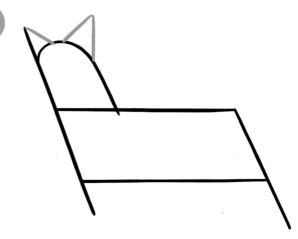

After erasing some lines, draw the
features and some furry lines.

FERRET

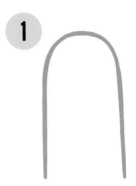

1

Start by drawing an upside-down U shape.

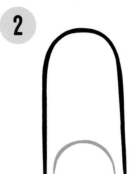

2

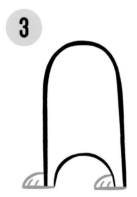

3

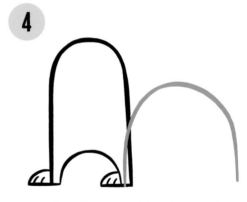

4

Another upside-down U shape makes the back of the ferret's body.

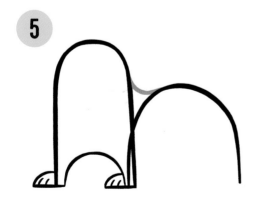

5

6

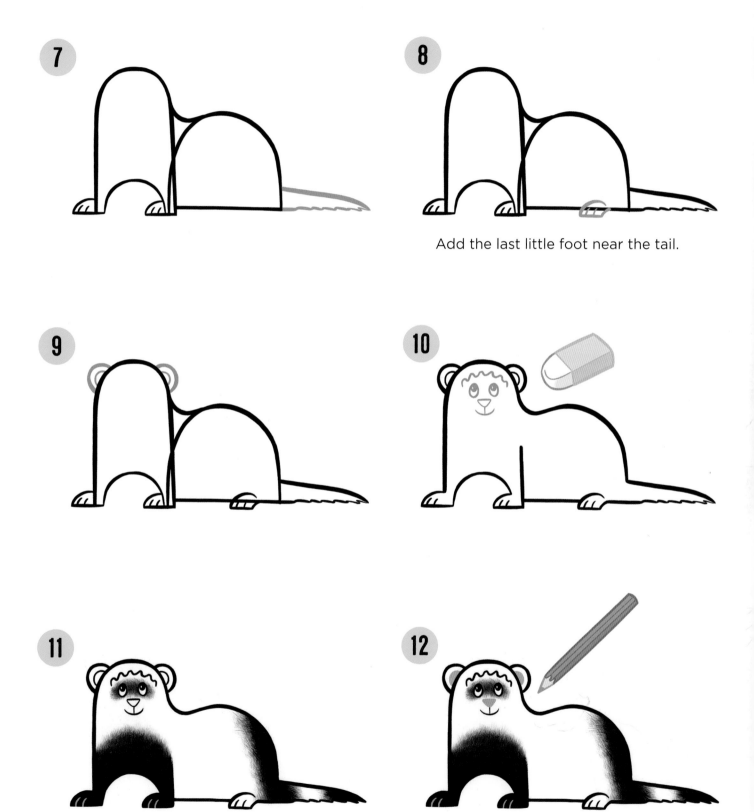

8 Add the last little foot near the tail.

Add some soft-looking fur using a black colored pencil. Color the nose and ears pink, and you're done!

GUINEA PIG

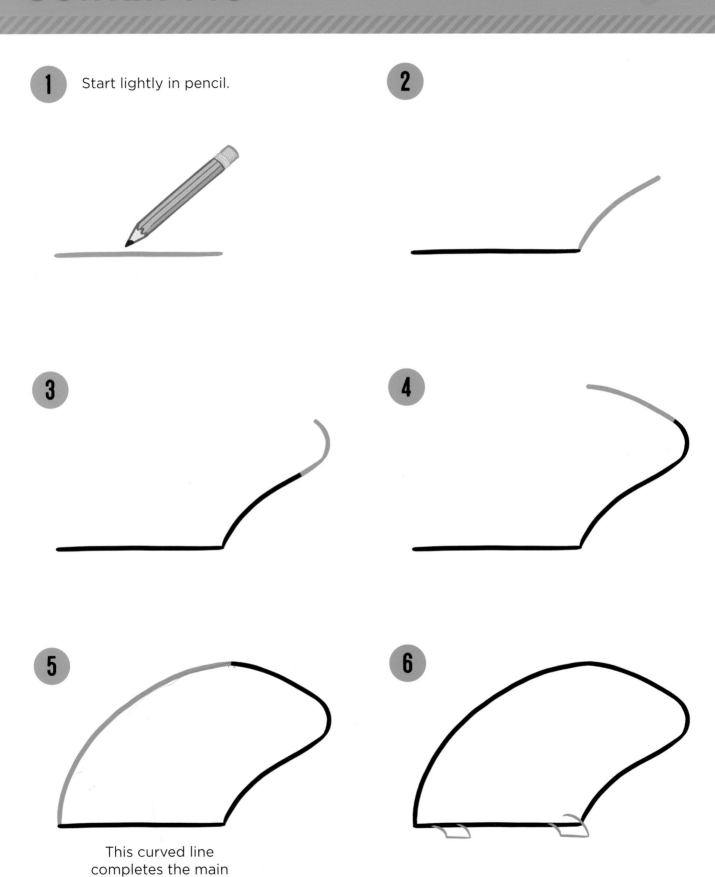

1 Start lightly in pencil.

2

3

4

5 This curved line completes the main body shape.

6

7

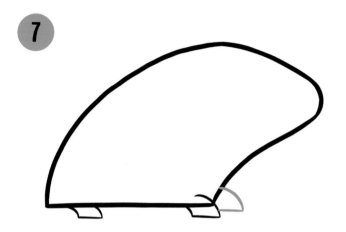

8

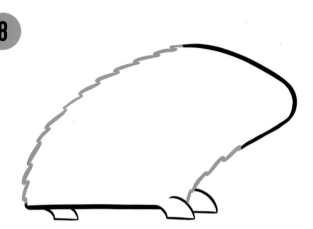

After erasing the lines you don't need, draw some furry lines.

9

10

11

Draw a ball for the guinea pig to play with!

12

Use light colored pencil strokes to make your guinea pig look soft and furry.

LIZARD

1

2

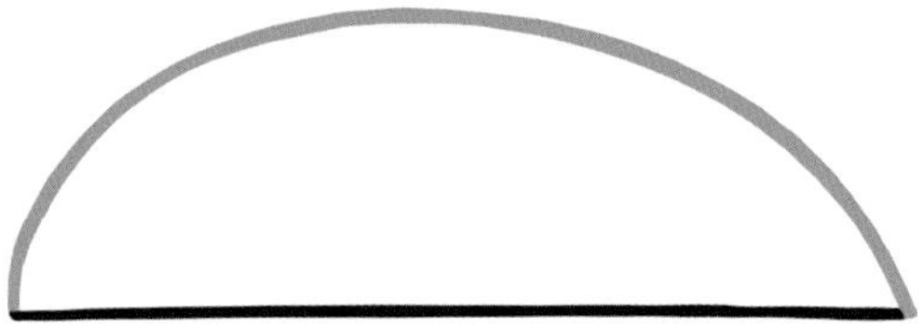

Start with a horizontal line and a curved line above it.

3

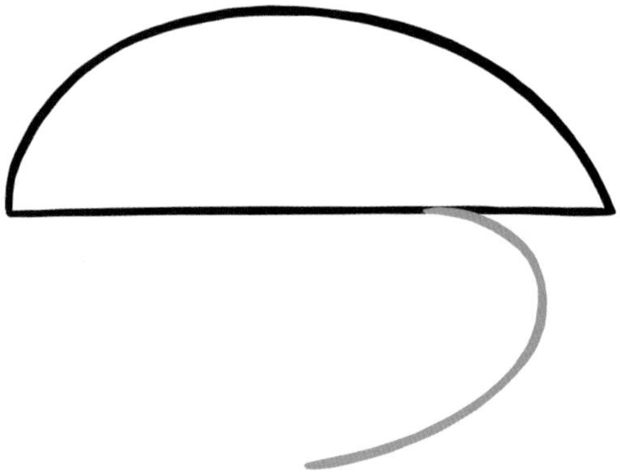

4

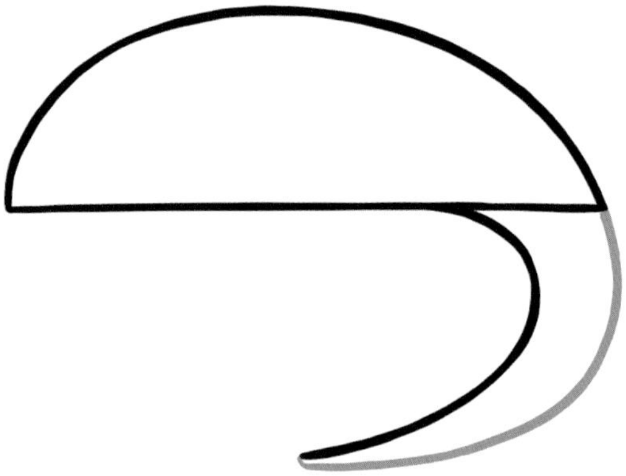

5

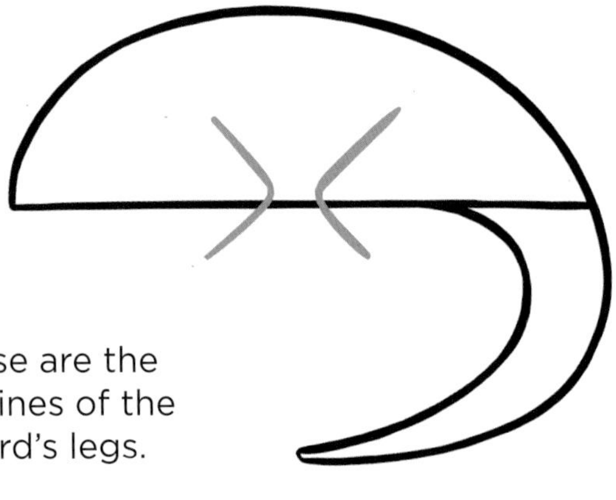

These are the
first lines of the
lizard's legs.

6

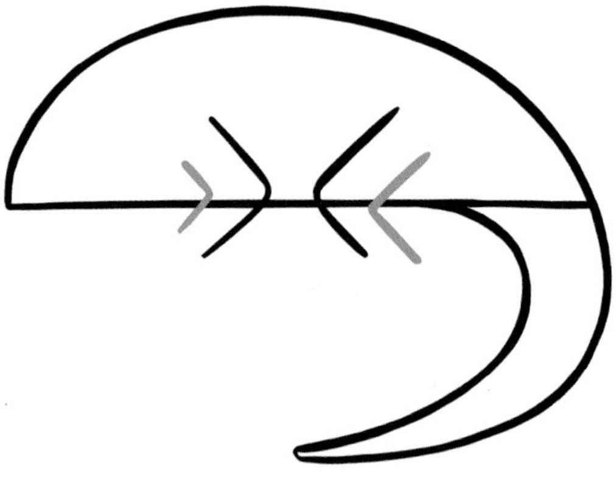

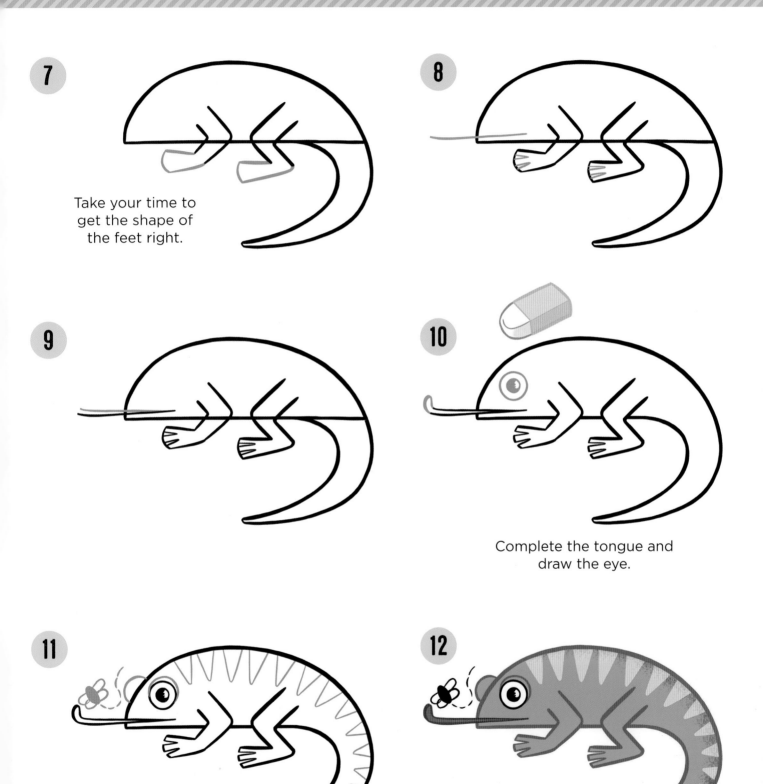

7 Take your time to get the shape of the feet right.

8

9

10 Complete the tongue and draw the eye.

11

12 Draw any pattern you like and add some bright colors.

SNAKE

1

2

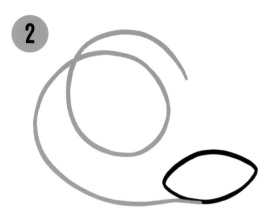

3

Take your time to draw a line that matches the first looping line.

4

5

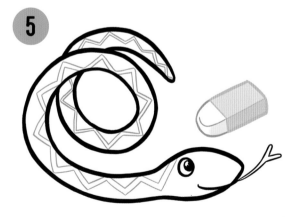

Erase the lines you don't need on the snake's body and draw its pattern.

6

Choose your own snake colors!

CHINCHILLA

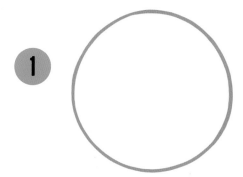

1 Start lightly in pencil with a nice big circle.

2

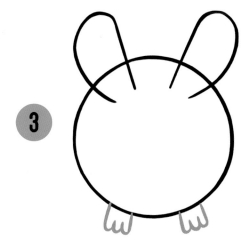

3

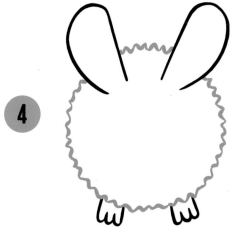

4 Erase the lines you no longer need and draw a furry line over the circle with a pen or pencil.

5

6

POT-BELLIED PIGLET

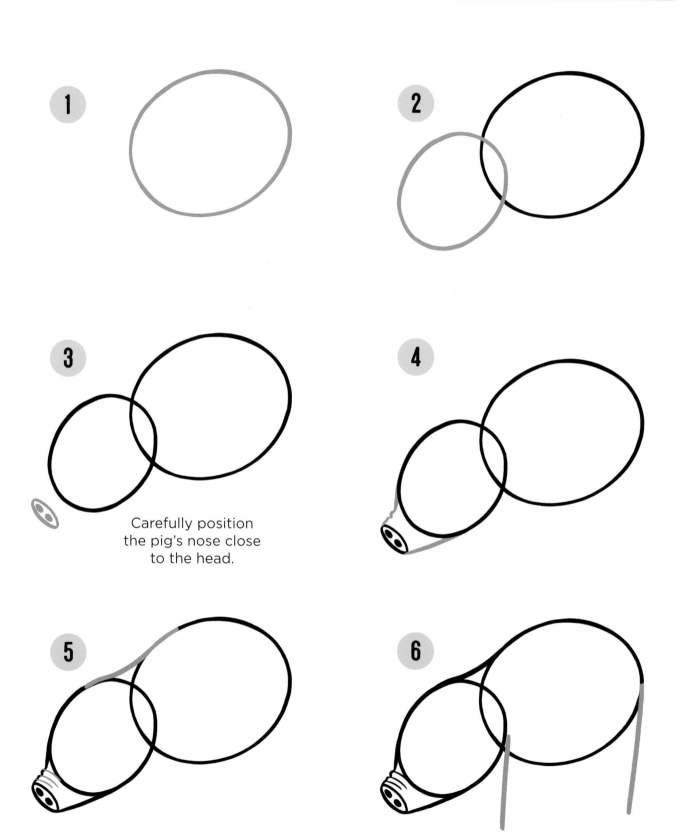

Carefully position the pig's nose close to the head.

7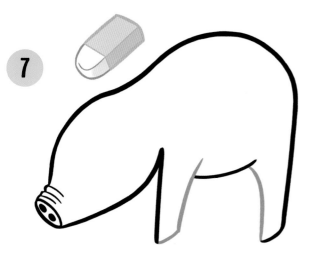

Finish the first two legs and
erase the lines you don't need.

8

9

10

11

12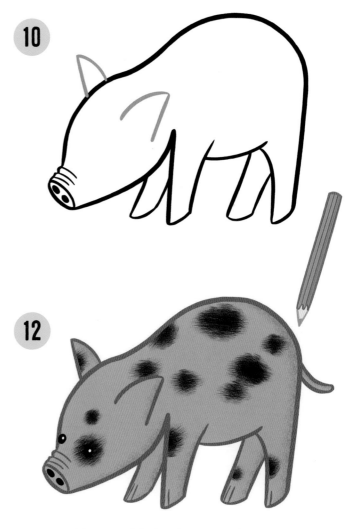

You could shade your pig one
color, or add a pattern.

SHORT-EARED RABBIT

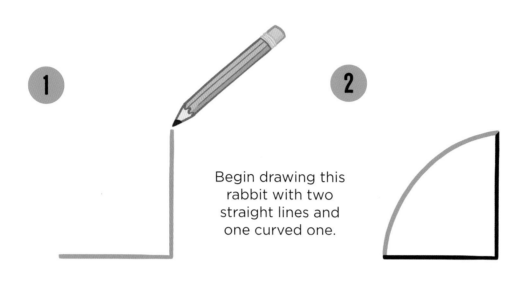

1

2

Begin drawing this rabbit with two straight lines and one curved one.

3

4

Make sure the head shape is nearly as wide as the body.

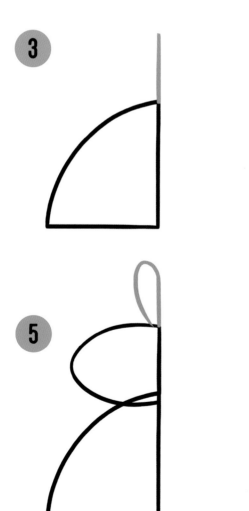

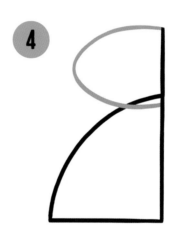

5

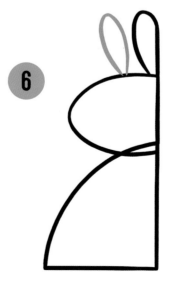

6

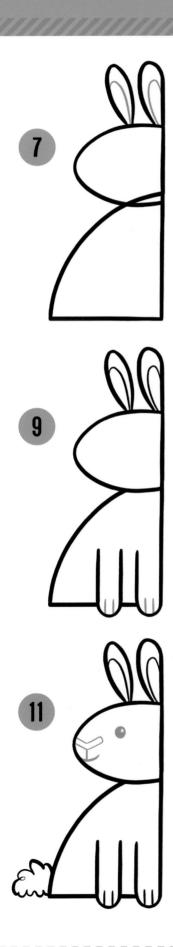

Add some color, but don't forget to leave some white patches.

TURTLE

1

2

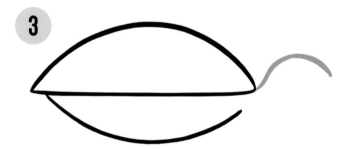

3

This curved line starts
the head shape.

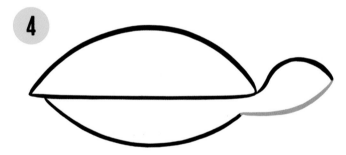

4

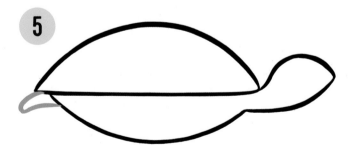

5

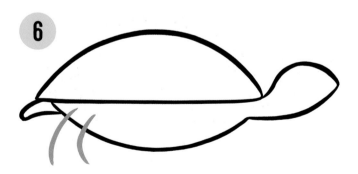

6

Take your time to get the leg
shapes right in this step and
the next.

7

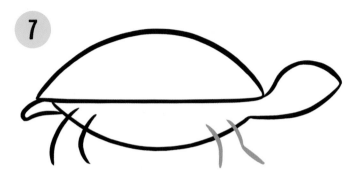

8

Erase the lines that cross through the legs. Then add the toes.

9

10

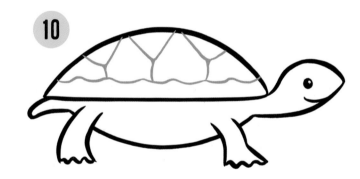

Design your turtle shell pattern.

11

Use wavy lines for the body pattern.

12

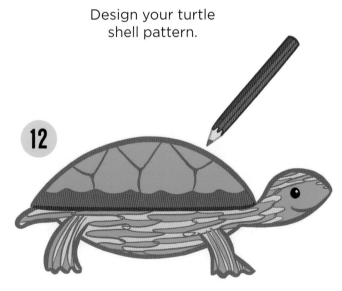

Also available in this series ...

I Can Draw: Wild Animals
ISBN: 978-1-60058-938-6

I Can Draw: Cats & Kittens
ISBN: 978-1-60058-958-4

I Can Draw: Everything Cute & Cuddly
ISBN: 978-1-60058-960-7

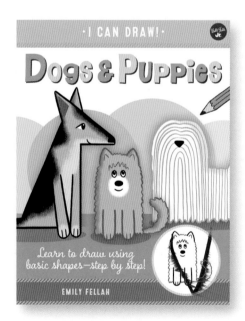

I Can Draw: Dogs & Puppies
ISBN: 978-1-60058-962-1

Visit www.QuartoKnows.com